BEYOND THE Veil

BEYOND THE *Veil*

Secrets from a Bridal Boutique

LORRAINE COXALL

To order additional copies of this book, contact:
Xlibris
NZ TFN: 0800 008 756 (Toll Free inside the NZ)
NZ Local: 9-801 1905 (+64 9801 1905 from outside New Zealand)
www.Xlibris.co.nz
Orders@Xlibris.co.nz
852324

CONTENTS

INTRODUCTION

Hello Reader. Welcome to the wonderful world of romance, love and marriage. It is my privilege to share with you a few true stories of the circumstances of some of my brides during my 30 yrs of business in the wedding industry. My career has operated over two countries and it has proved very rewarding both professionally and personally. Today I still have friends who started out as a bride and her Mum visiting for their first appointment. Sharing joy, excitement, and often tears will bond many people. For me, it has been a truly wonderful experience being part of so many lives and watching the evolving and changing wedding scene over this time.

I began my career really by accident. In the 1970s my daughter was married in a small country town about one hour's drive away from the nearest city. Her wedding was in a lovely church but the wedding reception was held in one of the local halls. This made it necessary for me to spend hours sewing bridal table skirtings, matching cake table skirtings, swags for draping the hall roof and walls, making ring cushions and coverings for a bridal table backdrop, and pew decorations. The hall looked stunning on the day, and all went well. Six months later I opened a wardrobe where all the wedding items were stored, and the thought crossed my mind "It would have been a lot easier to have been able to hire all these wedding extras"

Lightbulb moment
Start a wedding hire business. So I did just that.

For the first four years my business boomed and was very successful, then customers approached me regarding the possibility of stocking some wedding gowns for them to hire. *So I did that.* Then came the request for gowns to purchase. *So I did that.* This pattern continued over time until I had a Bridal Boutique that covered all bridal needs and also provided exceptional personal service for my clientele. Word of mouth spread, and this resulted in many clients that preferred to travel to me instead of purchasing from their local city shops. It was a really fun time for me, although I had to learn about the industry as I participated in it. Unfortunately, I made a few costly mistakes in dealing with suppliers along the way. Ignorance is not always bliss!

As time passed another local decided to open a bridal shop, but she chose to have her boutique in the nearest big city. So city brides were visiting the country boutique while the country brides visited the city boutique. It worked well for us and we often collaborated by sending clients to each other. However, after 20 years my life circumstances changed, and it was then that I decided to emigrate back to my birth country. I moved my business with me and spent a further ten years adjusting to another economy and new brides.

It was worth every minute of my time right up until I retired. Discussing my varied experiences with friends, I was prompted by them to share some of them with you. *So I'm doing just that.*

As these stories are all true and deal with real people and their families, I have respected the right to privacy of those mentioned by not using their names. Also not mentioned are the business names I have used or the countries I have worked in. I trust you enjoy the book under these conditions and thank you for sharing this trip back in time with me.

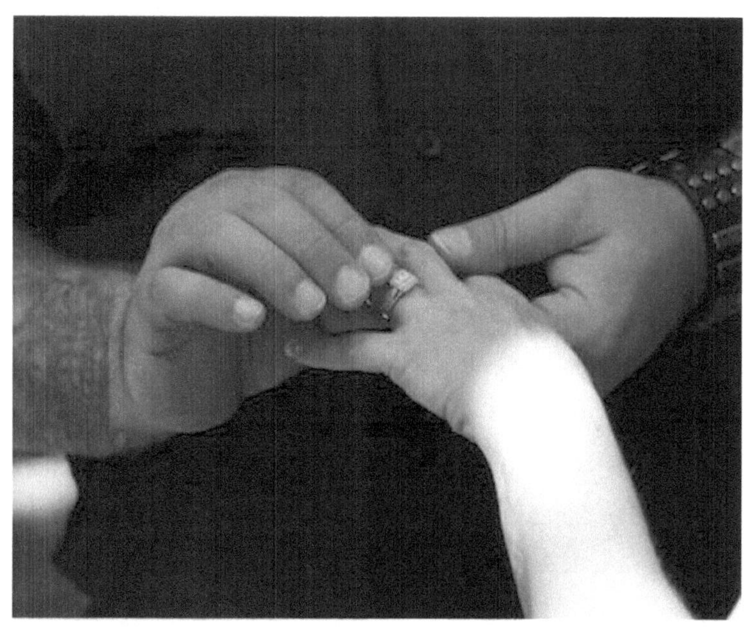

CHAPTER ONE

In The Beginning

Back in 1970, the parents of the couple usually shared the total cost of the wedding between the families. This gave them total veto rights to every part of the day as they were footing the bill. During these years, sex wasn't discussed openly, and the moral standard of the time was that the bride was a virgin on her wedding day.

This entitled her to wear a white wedding gown and veil to symbolize her purity and innocence. A lot of white was worn I remember, even though in reality the swinging sixties era was well-established and practised.

Bride A, a mature lady, visited the shop alone for the first time.. She looked to be aged around fifty, and she confirmed she had been married and then divorced. Now she had met a fabulous man who had personally chosen the very large diamond solitaire she wore on her engagement finger. All excited, she asked for my advice on what would be suitable for her second wedding. I was delighted to produce a lovely two-piece heavy cream elegant lace wedding suit for her. The suit top was constructed with cleverly shaped panels that defined the figure and had a fitted small peplum on the hip line. The slimline narrow skirt flowed down under the knee and the back kick pleat had an insert of pleated fabric. Bride A looked truly stunning as she had the height to carry it off and the design hid her slight plumpness. Bride A was amazed at how stunning she looked. However, she asked to try on more traditional gowns stating that her fiance hasn't ever been married and he wanted to see her as a traditional bride. So after making many suggestions, my bride chose for herself a particular gown that she requested her fiance be allowed to see on her. Another appointment was duly made, where I got to meet the groom (who was a distinguished-looking man) who obviously wanted his future wife to have the best. The hire gown of her choosing was paraded for viewing in front of the groom complete with jewellery and veil. He was obviously happy to say yes to the dress and so the wedding went ahead with this hire gown. I'm sure the couple were happy, but as the bridal consultant I had to remember that the customer is always right, -even when they are wrong. You see dear reader, the gown chosen was a real Bo Peep style with a corset bodice and a very full skirt. The skirt had big pick-up sweeps around the bottom hem with small bows decorating it. A young bride in her twenties with lovely skin could have stunned anyone in this gown. The style was way too young looking for my mature-skinned bride and the colour did not flatter her as much as the cream had. YES, she chose white for the second time around.

Bride B was outgoing and bubbly and very excited to be in the store with her mother after recently getting engaged to her high school boyfriend. Aged twenty, she was looking forward to celebrating her 21st birthday as a Mrs. During the visit she stated the wedding was to take place over the Xmas season. This was so overseas relatives could be free to travel to the event. It was an enjoyable visit with Mum participating fully in discussions on what type of gown she thought suited the bride. I advised the clients that the full-skirted princess-look ball gown had to be ordered within the next two months to ensure delivery before the Xmas wedding.

Two months later both clients returned and Mum pulled me aside for a quiet word. She said her mother had recently died, and as a result of funeral costs, they had personally had a money set back Therefore they were going to have a quiet smaller wedding with fewer frills and they wished to purchase another gown. They bought an existing gown of soft flowing chiffon off the sale rack in an off-white colour and left the store with me wishing them well

Ten months later some bridesmaids were in the store chatting, and as I served them they mentioned Bride B by name. They commented that she had a 3-month-old beautiful baby boy, and wasn't it a shame how her parents made her have a rushed family-only wedding because she was pregnant. Even her friends hadn't been invited apparently. Someone else commented that their religion had strict rules about sex before marriage. I was sad for the bride who had her dream wedding crushed. I took comfort in knowing she had the man she loved and a beautiful healthy child. I hope all went well for them in their marriage despite their families!

Bride C was a quiet shy bride and most of the talking was done by her five bridesmaids. They were outgoing and chatty but obviously really good friends to the bride who was in her mid-twenties. The girls had been besties during school days and still were obviously. Bride C made it clear that she wanted a simple plain elegant gown and after a fun 2 hours she settled on an Aline small train gown with one simple row of beading on the bodice. She was happy to find it in the budget rack and bought it that day. On subsequent visits, I sold her the five bridesmaid dresses and all the accessories for the wedding party, which the Bride insisted on paying for.

The bridesmaid's gowns were a slim line midnight blue chiffon floaty style and they looked amazing all together. I did comment to the bride that she had paid four times more for her bridesmaids than she had chosen to spend on her own gown. A quiet smile and assurance that she loved her gown was the reply.

Bride C brought in her wedding photos to show me after the wedding and one shot stood out. They were all standing slightly sideways in a line along a beach railing and with the sunny beach scene and the bridesmaids blue and the white bride, it looked spectacular! When I commented that it was my favourite, the bride offered it to me for posting on my bridal shop photo wall. I gladly accepted. To my amazement, the Bride said she had only one regret about her wedding. When I said, in dismay, that there shouldn't have been any regrets surely, she said she wished she had gone for a fancier wedding gown! She felt she was overshadowed by the five bridesmaids in her photos. Considering the money she had spent on them all I could relate, as her gown did look very simple in the photos. I consoled her by reminding her that her gown was a true reflection of her own personality and that all brides have a special glow on the day that no one else can ever match! She was a beautiful bride and a lovely person and I hope over the years, when she looks back at photos, that regret won't still be there.

Bride D was a lovely blond, tall and slender with an enthusiastic manner. On her first visit, she chatted about her likes and her fiance. I couldn't help but notice multiple gold rings on every finger of her hands, plus the gold ankle bracelet and a fancy gold toe ring. While so much jewellery on one so young was a bit unusual, I thought perhaps she had inherited some of it. It was a pleasure to have her fall in love with a $5000 Haute Couture designer gown. She paid a third deposit in cash and then promised to pay it off by the end of the month True to her word she came back, again with a cash payment! Over the next few weeks, she popped in to order her veil and wedding shoes and even to purchase more jewellery for her three bridesmaids, paying with cash. Intrigued, I asked her what her fiance did for a living. She said he was a self-employed electrician who worked really long hours and was often away on business.

Over several months Bride D added to the spending by outfitting the bridesmaids with their gowns also. Again all cash payments. Obviously, she was my best customer that year for wedding sales as money seemed abundant and she didn't mind spending it. We had no issues with any aspect of the wedding and apparently it went off without a hitch. During this time my son, who worked as a prison correctional officer, came home one day and asked me a question. "Mum, do you know who the fiance of your latest client was?" I looked puzzled and confessed I had never met him. Son grinned widely, and said he had that day incarcerated the man after he was convicted of multiple drug deals.

I was very shaken and upset to realise that the money spent on the wedding came from illegal activities. No wonder the Bride has so much genuine jewellery to wear. Unbeknown to me I had helped to launder drug money! My moral code was outraged, but there was nothing I could do to change anything. I hope the couple did pay for their choices as life went on. Karma will happen eventually.

CHAPTER TWO

Whose Wedding Is This Anyway?

Weddings are supposed to be about the engaged couple committing to a lifetime together. This is all about the couple and their future blended families. However, everything does not always flow smoothly with families during the preparations.

Bride E had a dominating mother who gave her opinion on everything about the forthcoming wedding in loud tones. The Bride didn't look like she even wanted to be in the store when they made their first visit. Switched on to these types of situations. I had my assistant involve the mother in discussions on the type of venue and what the mother envisioned as a bridal gown to suit the type of ceremony. Then they discussed the mother of the bride's outfit for her and the best time to take photos etc. Meantime I had the chance to ask the bride what SHE hoped to wear for her wedding, and armed with this info, I quickly sorted out similar gowns to her description to start the fitting process.

During the fittings, mother tried to take over. She pulled gowns down off the racks for the bride to try on. Our Bride didn't like the styles and knew they would not suit her. They didn't, but to help pacify Mum, she tried them on. When my bride gave two thumbs up, a very big smile and a head nod when I put one designer gown on her, I knew before we opened the curtain to mother that this was the Bride's gown.

I discussed with the bride in front of Mum the designer's credentials, the way the gown was constructed, why it suited her so well compared to others she had tried on, and as the piece de resistance, there was a promotional discount on this style at that time. Mum gave the bride her opinion about the bargain and how suitable the gown was. The Bride (to her credit) acted doubtful, but then let her Mum persuade her to buy. A win-win for all.

The following day I received a big bouquet of flowers and a hug from the Bride for helping her buy the gown she really really loved. She explained her mother had never had a church wedding, and so she was living out her dream through her daughter. Understanding the reason behind her Mum's behavior helped the daughter enjoy her wedding despite unwanted opinions! Yes, I did get to add the photo of her and her Mum (looking elegant in a shot outside the church) to our bridal wall. They all really did look happy that day.

Bride F came from a certain ethnicity in our local area. My initial dealings with this culture were a learning experience! All the women were extremely well dressed and dripped with heavy gold jewelry. The women apparently all lived under their menfolk's domination and were treated as display objects and possessions. The menfolk made the decisions and the women had to go along with them. Status mattered to the men. Part of this show of status was the custom for the newlyweds to have their first new home built by the bride's parents very close to the family home. This home was the wedding gift to the couple and the home was fully furnished by the groom's parents. Neither member of the couple had any input into their new home or its location. On an annual basis, trips back to their original birth country were made and multiple amounts of gold jewelry were purchased and bought back. Every item was purchased to impress or outdo a neighbour.

Given this constant display of wealth, I found it difficult to understand why the Bride's mother kept trying to push me to lower the gown price. When I refused to lower the price, I was addressed verbally in their language with great passion. I understood not a word. It was obvious that Mother wasn't happy with me though!

To put a stop to the situation I tried a strategy. I acted as though I thought that price was their only concern. Comments about gowns perhaps being outside their budget, or perhaps a cheaper gown might appeal, or did they wish to look at the cheaper option of hiring, quickly put a stop to the haggling

Bride F spoke excellent English and was very pleasant to deal with all the way through. Her mother was obviously still annoyed at not getting her way regarding the discount. Hoping no doubt to find fault with me, the mother **lay down on the floor** to eye-check whether my recently pinned-up hem on the chosen bridal gown was level! The Bride was so embarrassed at her behavior but said nothing to Mum. I got a whispered apology from the bride as they left the shop. Amused, I recounted the incident to my dressmaker to warn her that the hem alterations might be inspected again after completion. *They were.* Mother once again lay down on the floor, but this time she received a real tongue lashing in the native dialect from the mortified bride. I'm glad I didn't understand a word!

Despite my not allowing discounts I had many clients from this ethnicity over the years. I did enjoy all the brides who shopped with me though I never learned a single word of their native tongue. Fortunately, for me, all the brides spoke excellent English.

Bride G was unfortunate to have a bridesmaid's problem right from the first visit to choose her gown. One of the three bridesmaids expressed her opinions on the bridal gowns without asking the Bride how she felt or what she thought. Since this particular bridesmaid's opinions were negative, the whole appointment went downhill quickly.

The two other bridesmaids try really hard to assist and interact with the bride, as did I. The Bride became so tense that she decided to make a private appointment for just her and her Mum for another day and having done so they all left.

On her next visit, Bride G had a really fun time. She shared memories of her courtship, the proposal and what they were hoping to achieve after their wedding. It was lovely to see her excited and happy, and she did fall in love with a gown that day and ordered it. Her sparkle died when she made an appointment for her bridesmaids to visit to try on gowns. She informed me that her future sister-in-law was the opinionated bridesmaid we had already met. According to the Bride, she was demanding and inconsiderate and liked to be in the spotlight. We discussed the colour choice for the bridesmaids and Bride G said her favorite was Dusky pink or a Rose shade. I promised to sort some styles in the chosen colour for the bridesmaid's visit.

D-day arrived and Bride and bridesmaids came into the store. I had several styles in the colours as promised and two bridesmaids really looked good in them. Sister-in-law declared, without even trying a gown on, that she would look hideous in that colour. Also, she didn't like the styles, (so carefully chosen by me to flatter all three differently shaped girls,) and demanded that she be allowed to choose her own style and colour. The colour blue and style she chose for herself did look nice on her body, but it didn't suit the shape so well of the other two bridesmaids. When asked to consider her choice again for a style that would suit all of them better, she flatly refused. We were told that as the groom's sister, she was the most important bridesmaid and they had to agree to what she had chosen. Bride G tried to make peace by agreeing to change the gowns to her blue colour, but said she needed a different style for her friends. She was told rudely that they would have to accept it or drop out of the bridal party. I had never heard anyone talk to a person in my shop in such a rude manner. To assist with the situation, I told the bride that it wasn't unusual to have a special bridesmaid sign the wedding register as a witness. This bridesmaid could wear a different style of gown to the others as it was an important honour. As long as the colours matched the styles didn't have to. Bride G leapt at this idea, her sister-in-law got the limelight and her way, and the other bridesmaids got a style more becoming to their body shapes.

Regretfully, the person who missed out on this solution was our lovely Bride, who didn't get to have her colour choice at her own wedding, I commend her for her restraint that day. She put her future relationship with her fiancé ahead of what she had dreamed of having on their special day. I am sure she would have made it a point to avoid her sister-in-law whenever possible after her marriage. I would, were I in her shoes.

One unusual event happened at a time when it was fashionable to have a local school Debutant ball every year. A mother turned up to investigate what styles I had on my rack for the upcoming Deb ball. She asked if she could take one home for her daughter to try on approval. I said it wasn't company policy, but that we could fit an appointment for the daughter after hours or even on a weekend to suit her timetable. Mother insisted that with her shift work and the daughter's schedule, this wouldn't be possible. As the customer was a complete stranger and I didn't like the vibe I was picking up on, I suggested she talk to the daughter and get back to me. Mother exited the store, and we didn't see her again.

Six months later I received a phone call from a gentleman who stated he owed me money on a wedding dress he believed his fiancé had purchased from me. I had no one on my books under the name he gave for the fiancé and suggested he had the wrong bridal store perhaps. He then went on to describe the interior of my shop and its street location and stated that every time they had driven past, his fiancé had teased him about having her gown stored so close but not for him to see! He was adamant that he had dropped her off at my store. When I again said no sale had been made to his fiancé the penny dropped for the groom. It turned out they had had a fancy dinner on the previous Friday night together and the fiancé had stated she was visiting a friend over the long weekend. When he visited her residence after the weekend, it was empty of all her belongings, and she had disappeared completely! As he was ringing around the so-called wedding suppliers, he was finding out that nothing had been organized for a wedding at all. He, however, had been giving the fiancé money for 12 months towards the cost of their wedding. It was apparent to us both that he had been scammed big time!

While on the phone, I described the Mother who wanted to take a Deb gown out of the store. Her description matched his fiancé. I was lucky not to be scammed out of a gown by this con artist, but still felt for the poor man who had lost not only money but his trust and faith in a loving relationship.

CHAPTER THREE

Bridezillas Are Real!

The term Bridezilla can be interpreted differently according to each individual perspective. As a Bridal consultant, it meant one thing to me. A client who was demanding and impossible to please whatever extra services were done free of charge. Fortunately, they were few in number though always memorable.

Bride H visited alone for her first appointment. She had pictures of several gowns that she liked. So, I had a guide to show her styles with some of the features she liked actually on her body. During our chat she said she had been living with her fiancé for five years without a marriage proposal. She had taken matters into her own hands by issuing an ultimatum. Marry me or I move on! This statement should have sent alarm bells off in my head, but it didn't of course. The result of her visit was that we found several different gowns that she liked individual parts off, so I suggested she meet my dressmaker and get a quote to have her own style constructed from what suited her. She was very forthright in what she desired with the dressmaker but did accept her suggestion as to what fabric to use for the gown. Pleading ignorance of fabrics, she handed the dressmaker the responsibility of sourcing samples for her to choose from. This was done for her by my dressmaker, who made phone calls and travelled to another city free of charge to collect samples Bride H didn't like them, so it was a situation of repeating the whole process, which was unpaid time and effort. On the third attempt the Bride chose a particular fabric but again told the dressmaker to order the amount needed. At this point, the dressmaker protected herself by having the Bride sign off on the issued quote and had her pay for the fabric in advance. Bride H then decided to bring her four bridesmaids in to try on styles in the store. Again, the Bride had all the say and the bridesmaid's helpful suggestions as to what they liked were totally ignored. All of them left the shop with glum faces as the Bride stated she knew what they needed! During many fittings for her gown, Bride H changed her mind about the gown neckline, and then the style of the floaty sleeve, and then about how full the skirt needed to be. This involved the dressmaker making more and more trips for fabric and redoing what she had already sewn. It also added to the sewing time and meant more time for extra fittings. Eventually, the gown was finished but of course, Bride H had the nerve to comment that had the dressmaker been more skilled it wouldn't have taken so long! Obviously, she was totally unaware that the style pattern had to be drafted by the dressmaker before she even cut the fabric to begin the sewing process.

When Bride H was told the cost of the finished gown, she went ballistic! There had been extra hours of sewing and material added, but not the travel or drafting pattern costs of course. She berated the dressmaker so much that the poor woman was on the point of tears. Bride H refused to pay anything more than the original quote. The poor dressmaker caved under the pressure and accepted the lower payment just to see the back of the client. As anybody in this situation would. When I heard about this horrid behavior, I came up with a solution to prevent the situation from happening ever again. A stamp was made to be added to all the future dressmaker quotes, saying that any alterations to the design of any sort would need to have another quote given and accepted.

Several months after this wedding one of the bridesmaids came into the shop as a newly engaged bride. Of course, she mentioned she wasn't going to treat her bridesmaids as she had been treated by Bride H. Apparently, the Bride had told them she would pay for their bridesmaid's dresses, but they had to let the Bride choose the style. I didn't see the photos of the wedding party but was informed the style and colour looked dowdy It was felt by those in the bridal party that the Bride had done it on purpose so that she would look better than anyone else. Given that the bride was a biggish person, and the bridesmaids weren't, I could believe this. The wedding day was unpleasant for the bridesmaids as apparently, the Bride hadn't done as she said and expected the bridesmaids to pay for their gowns! The friendships, of course, fell apart after the wedding, due to their treatment. I now think I know why Bride H didn't get a romantic proposal.

I would be very surprised if her marriage survived for any length of time.

Bride I also had been living with her partner for seven years and again she also gave the ultimatum to her partner. I notice she didn't choose to make a romantic proposal to him regarding marriage. Perhaps she feared a no answer! This lady was in her early thirties and clearly had a mindset directed toward her own wants. She tried on several styles in-store but stated that her mother personally knew my dressmaker, so the wedding party would be getting the wedding gown and bridesmaids' gowns made, She was happy to purchase jewelry and her veil through me though, so that worked well Over the coming months, I heard how all out the wedding was to be, The service was to be held in the stunning gardens of one of the top city hotels. The hotel gave the couple the use of the bridal suite free for one night as part of their deal. There were six bridesmaids' gowns, one bridal gown and one Mother of the Bride gown for the dressmaker to sew. Bride I was happy to tell how her wedding cake had TEN tiers with linking bridges between them and a bridal couple and doves all done in icing. It sounded stunning. Also, she had hired a local horse and carriage to transport her to the venue but then had also hired limousines for the drive to scenic outlooks for photos. I believe that the term Dream wedding was certainly covered here.

When the bride picked up her gown and bridesmaids, the dressmaker expected to be paid on the day after all her months of work. Bride I informed her that mom would be paying for it, so as the mother still had a fitting to go to, the dressmaker didn't worry. At Mums fitting she said payment would be made via the internet which the dressmaker was happy with. Mums payment came through overnight for her gown but nothing else. The dressmaker waited two weeks after the wedding and then contacted Mum regarding payment. Imagine her shock when a bewildered Mum said the wedding was supposed to have been paid for by the couple. Due to them being away on their honeymoon Mum couldn't contact the Bride but would certainly get it sorted out as soon as she could.

Two weeks later the bride's mom rang the dressmaker in tears. Through sobs, she said she had just heard from the groom who stated the wedding was off! Bride I had finished the wedding celebrations with a fireworks display over the garden area before heading upstairs to the bridal suite. There she proceeded to tell her new husband that the wedding was a mistake, and she would be getting an annulment immediately. She grabbed her bags and exited the hotel for parts unknown. The distraught groom had ended up sedated in hospital for several days after a complete breakdown and hadn't been able to locate his wife in the time after. He was of the opinion his Bride had just wanted the full wedding experience and not the marriage. Given how extravagant the wedding had been with all the bells and whistles, I think I agree.

The sad part was that the bride's parents had to remortgage their home in their twilight years to pay all the bills for their daughter's spectacle wedding. It impacted their friendship with the groom's family of course, and their heartache at the behavior of the daughter must have been huge, I felt for the parents having to explain to the creditors, and others, the situation. I'm sure Bride I would win an award for Bridezillar of the year if there was such a thing.

Bride J came into the store while a sale was on. I estimated her to be in her forties and she stated she hadn't been married before. As a first-time bride, I took her through the usual bride protocols of buying a gown from the rack as compared to ordering one in, about the time frames for organizing a wedding, the payment options for purchasing, and the legal agreement pertaining to purchases, We then visited the sale rack as her budget apparently was limited. After trying on several gowns, she fell in love with a coloured one and purchased it with her credit card. She asked me to hold the gown out the back of my shop until she could store it with a friend. I agreed happily.

Three months later, Bride J contacted me to say she thought she had made a hasty decision and could she come and try on more gowns. I wanted her to be happy and agreed to this. She had a fun time but decided the gown already purchased was THE one.

Six weeks later I started to get photos of bridal gowns from Bride J asking if I thought the different styles would suit her, I replied politely that while they would possibly suit, she shouldn't be looking at other styles since she had purchased her gown already, I pointed out there were new styles always coming out and she should stop looking as it was not necessary. A few weeks later Bride J rang to say she had seen a new style on my website and could she please visit the store to try it on. Of course, she wanted to exchange her previous choice for the new gown once she saw it on. I pointed out that it was nearly twice the price of her earlier one, but she said she could find the money for the three-monthly payments that would be necessary.

Reluctantly I agreed to exchange the gowns but it involved a lot of time redoing my inventory and the sales bookwork, and then setting up the new sale. Part of the second payment was paid early, but the balance wasn't paid by the date due. When I tried to phone the bride, it said the number wasn't in service and emails went unanswered. I was very concerned that she might have been in an accident, but I didn't have her work details to check on her.

A few days later a man entered the shop and introduced himself as the best man for the Bridal couple. He stated the groom had just lost his job, and that the couple had major car repairs to find money for. He was to be their Best Man, and he suggested that as a wedding gift, he would take over the money owning by making fortnightly payments.

He couldn't meet the time frame for the full amount, but I said I was prepared to extend the payment time if payments were regularly made. They were, though it took months of payments.

Bride J also turned up during this time to purchase her wedding veil and more expensive jewelry, which went onto the account. I felt sorry for the best man.

After 11 months when the time was approaching for the wedding gown alterations to be organized, I was surprised to see Bride J outside the shop door making a phone call while her Matron of honour marched into the premises. She demanded that the Bride be reimbursed the full payment of all monies as she didn't wish to use her purchases for her wedding. I was totally speechless as the woman waved the consumer rights act in front of my face and threatened legal action, I informed her I would be consulting my solicitor regarding the matter and would get back to her. It turned out that, despite the fact that legal rights were on my side, the cost of proving the matter would be more disadvantages with the bad publicity for the business. It would be more prudent to provide a refund. Seething I contacted the Bride to say I would refund the monies, but it would only be the portion she had paid previously that would get to her. By law, the rest had to be returned to the Best man's account. She didn't like this, but I won that argument.

If you think that ended the matter. I regret to inform you it didn't. One month after her wedding date Bride J was written up, with a wedding photo attached, in an article in our local paper. She espoused how easy it was to buy the perfect wedding gown **online** with the right research. Some customers retailers can do without.

CHAPTER FOUR

Second Time Around

Second- time brides are usually more relaxed than when they got married the first time, I personally have found. They frequently refer to their first wedding as a big fuss or production. Older, wiser and knowing themselves better, they opt for more of an intimate personal experience the second time. Many chose to wear coloured gowns for these weddings, and they often chose a gown style that allows them to be able to wear it again later for other functions.

Bride K made her appointment to visit alone for the first time. She was relaxed and happy about her second wedding. She stated she didn't want the fuss or drama that usually went with the first wedding, which she had already experienced. Hence her appointment was without her mother or two best friends. We had an interesting 2 hours sorting out some styles she liked, and the gown that she really loved, During the conversation she told me her story, Apparently, in her high school years she had a good friendly relationship with a boy at school who she felt was her true soulmate. Romance blossomed and they dated after leaving school for three years. Aged 20 and 21 the couple planned to become engaged, but the mother had a different opinion. She explained to her daughter that she hadn't travelled to broaden her horizons nor dated anyone else. According to Mum, she needed to live life more before settling down.

Eventually Mum made the bride doubt her decision and the couple parted company.

Bride K travelled overseas, fell in love with the country she visited and ended up with a career that she loved there, Time passed, and she dated others. After a two-year courtship, she agreed to marry her boyfriend of the time. She did confess to me that she wondered if he was the right one during the engagement and the night before their wedding! After 13 years of marriage and having given birth to two boys, she realized she wasn't happy and so the marriage ended. Divorced, she returned to her home country with her boys, and while walking along the local beachfront one day she literally bumped into her high school love. Over a coffee catch-up, he revealed he had lost his wife to cancer and that his biggest regret was that they were childless because of it. Yes, reader, her current fiancé was her first love!

Bride K said it was comical to hear her mother rave about her fiancé and how well-suited they were as a couple, and how they were true soul mates. She laughed as she warned me, I would hear it all on their next visit together. I certainly did hear the fiancé's virtues extolled at length by a beaming very happy Mum on the next visit. Mum was so happy to see her daughter in the ivory wedding gown Bride K had fallen in love with, an made it obvious how delighted she was with the whole wedding idea. Everybody was so happy and excited, especially the bride.

I'm sure the separation of this couple over all the years only added a depth of appreciation to their marriage. They had a loving bonded family unit together and the knowledge that they had been given this second chance at happiness. Their story would make a lovely Walt Disney movie I'm sure.

Bride L first visited my shop as a bridesmaid for her friend. At the time she had a two-year-old and was heavily pregnant with her second child. As the wedding was months away, we knew she would be in the bridal party regardless of her current condition. After being in the store and helping her friend decide on the perfect gown, the bridesmaids stated that should she get married again she would be buying through my store. With a very big smile, I pointed out that would probably not be happening due to her being a pregnant married woman already. You can imagine my dismay when the bridesmaid explained that her husband had walked out on her when she informed him of the second unplanned pregnancy. Apparently, his words were "I can't cope with this"! It transpired he had been abusive with words and fists during their marriage, as her bride-friend interrupted to tell me. She expressed her opinion that her bridesmaid was much better off without him at home. So here was this lovely young woman, with only family support, facing the future alone with two children and a divorce ahead. All I could do was hug her and wish her well.

Two years later Bride L entered my shop with a big smile and flashed her new engagement ring. Her first words were" I told you I would buy my gown with you". Delighted to see her, I asked for the details about her children, and the man responsible for the new ring. They had met at a social gathering and got chatting. This resulted in a date and then more, leading to the engagement. They were both locals, divorced with two children each. Bride L happily told me how wonderful her fiancé was to her and her children, and how well all four children got on together. She said it was so nice to be treated so well by the man she was marrying, and she really glowed as she talked about him. They were going to make the ceremony about blending the families, and each child would therefore have a special role to manage on the day. The couple were in the process of obtaining a mortgage together to buy a new home, and so they had decided to forego the honeymoon to save capital. They hoped to enter the home after the wedding for the first time with the children as a new family. It sounded like such a lovely beginning for them all, and I got a bit emotional thinking about it.

I never got to meet the groom, but the children visited with Bride L at different times, They were typical children, active, curious, vocal and sometimes cheeky, but so obviously excited to be part of a wedding for the first time. It was an enjoyable experience having them in the store. I got photos of the wedding sent to me with a lovely thank you note from Bride L, which went up on the display wall of the shop

Eighteen months later, I was shocked to receive the news that Bride L had separated from her husband. It appeared the facade of a loving caring man had soon disappeared after the marriage. Domestic violence this time resulted in the hospitalization of Bride L on two occasions. The children were taken into care as a result. I was told Bride L had left the marital home and was currently living in her parent's home with her own children.

My heart ached to hear this story, as she had believed in him and their future together. I wondered at the fates which had put two dysfunctional men in her life in such a short time. I sincerely hope her future has become better and safer in the last few years.

Bride M came into the store rather hesitantly. As a senior citizen, she had never expected to be looking at wedding attire in her later years. She shared with me that she had been widowed for 20 yrs., she had loving caring children, many friends and lots of activities. Her passion was to travel on cruises apparently. It was on a long cruise she had befriended a man in her age group, and they spent a lot of time laughing and having fun together. After the cruise, they dated and now she was engaged to him. She said it was lovely to have someone to share and laugh with every day after being on her own for so long.

The couple had decided to have a simple garden wedding with only her family present. The groom was divorced with no children so would only have his close friends there. I was delighted to hear the celebrant was a close friend of mine, and I told the Bride I would like the friend to take a picture of the couple on the day if she was happy to agree. She gave her permission willingly. I suggested to Bride M that she purchase a full evening gown for the wedding so that she could wear it again on her next cruise. I was informed that would be in Greece for the honeymoon. I promptly offered to carry her bags but was told three would be a crowd!

Her wedding gown was a dark blue chiffon empire style, with a fitted crossed bodice lightly beaded. The skirt gathered softly in the center front and back panel over an A-line shaped skirt, and the sleeves were a floating bell shape. She looked really lovely in her choice and left the shop with a big smile.

Sometime after her wedding date I had coffee with my celebrant friend and asked to see their wedding photo. It was a nice close-up shot of the wedding couple looking so happy together. Sentimental as always, I commented to the celebrant how nice it was for them to have found each other in their later years.

My friend gave me a strange look, then commented that it was a pity it wouldn't last beyond the honeymoon! She stated that after filing the marriage details with the court, it was proven that his divorce hadn't been finalized, and he was actually a Bigamist! When I questioned my friend re the legalities, she said that no marriage is actually legal until filed with the courts. An interesting fact that means all newly married couples aren't legally married until a few days after the wedding ceremony! When I questioned how the groom could produce a divorce certificate as required legally before the marriage, she explained that the laws can differ between countries. A divorce can be legal for one applicant but not be recognized in the country of the other. What a situation to be in!

What a horrid shock and upset would await my couple on their return from Greece though. I never did find out whether it was unintentional bigamy or deliberate on the groom's part. Nor, unfortunately, do I know how it all was resolved.

Chapter Five
Till Death Us Do Part

The words "Till death do us part" had been used in religious ceremonies for several centuries.

As times have changed from the more traditional formal weddings, these words have been dropped from the vows in many instances. However, the meaning has been very poignant, regretfully for many of my customers and myself.

Bride N was young but very happy when she entered my shop on a

Friday. She had a wedding gown already purchased elsewhere but needed her hem length altered. She asked if I would do this for her and I agreed. After pinning the hemline, I assisted her with some jewelry and a veil to complete her bridal look. She stood in front of the shop mirror with a big smile and said to her attending bridesmaid "Just think, this is how he will see me next week" We all agreed she was a beautiful bride, and he would no doubt have tears in his eyes when he saw her. Theirs was a high school romance also, but I was informed both families were thrilled to see them together.

As the wedding was so close, I told Bride M that the alterations would be finished over the weekend, and she could collect her gown on Monday. We arranged she would collect it around seven in the evening, as she had a meeting after work that day. She would rush home for a shower and then come in for the final fitting

During the weekend an extreme weather system hit, deluging the streets with water and reducing visibility for driving to almost zero On Monday evening a full thunderstorm raged, so I expected to receive a phone call from my bride cancelling the appointment. It didn't happen. I assumed that maybe the storm had taken down the phone connections and that the bride would be in touch the next day. Tuesday morning at seven-thirty am my home phone rang. On answering, I was shocked to hear a crying bridesmaid telling me the bride had died as she stepped out of her shower the night before! Speechless I listened to the bridesmaid explain that she had been born with an inoperable brain tumor and that her death could have happened anywhere, anytime. This was the reason the families had been so happy for the couple getting married while young apparently. Dazed. I did the best I could to assist the bridesmaid with her grief by letting her talk about her friendship and closeness to Bride N.

Listening and sympathizing was all I could offer, but she had stopped crying by the time we finished the phone call

Wednesday was a very emotional day in the shop. The bridegroom, his parents and the bride's parents all turned up to collect the gown. They were going to bury the bride as a bride in all her unseen finery. Her groom was trying to say thank you for doing the gown hem through his tears. He looked so young and lost at that moment. Emotion caught up with us all and we shed tears together as a group.

Group hugs and someone's wisecrack comment helped stop the waterworks eventually.

As they all left my boutique, I couldn't help thinking of the bride's comment about her groom seeing her as a bride, and my comment on him having tears in his eyes. Regretfully for all concerned, this would happen but not in the manner we all envisioned.

Bride O had her bridesmaids enter the store on her behalf. All five of them were outgoing and friendly but on a mission. They had come to inform me that their friend was dying of cancer, was in a long-term relationship, and was a Mum to two boys from a previous relationship. Her fiancé also had two boys and it was the bride's wish to see them joined as a family, as she knew they would be loved and cared for after her demise. The Bridesmaid told me that the local community had rallied around and raised $15000 for the family to travel overseas to visit the bride's family, while she was between treatments and still well enough to travel. They made an appointment date for the bride's visit and then exited the store stating they would all be back

Bride O was obviously tired on her first visit and did look pale, but she was really positive about her forthcoming wedding and her bridesmaids were fantastic! They teased her about looking like a historic maiden on the day, Demure and pale and with a wig of flowing hair entwined with flowers. This did make the bride laugh, but she commented that there would have to be a wig worn. Despite the sadness of the situation, that appointment and all the subsequent visits always had laughter attached. The Bridesmaids were out to make the whole event special and fun obviously.

We were all dismayed when Bride O underwent aggressive therapy just three weeks out from the wedding. When she came into the store one week out from the wedding day, to finalize small things, she had lost her hair and her voice box had been affected so much that she could barely whisper. Once again, the Bridesmaids were there in force and carried the day with assurances and laughter. Coincidentally, the bride had chosen a gown that had a corset laced back for herself and also for the Bridesmaids. Lacing up takes about 20 minutes per gown. The Bridesmaids went into a panic about how long it would take to do this on the wedding day. I pointed out that everybody would do it at the same time. All they needed to do was form a circle and do the lacing of the gown in front of them. We all had a practice run in the store, so they felt confident to do so on the big day.

According to the Bridesmaids, the wedding day was joyous and so meaningful for everybody there. The whole day had shared love and laughter, and of course some tears, but the couple were so happy, and the weather was just perfect. I asked what type of cancer was affecting the bride and was told it was in her lungs. Her occupation required the cleaning of work surfaces with chemicals at day's end, and it was supposed that over the years she had inhaled the fumes.

A non-smoker and non-drinker, the bride had tried to live a healthy lifestyle. Life can be needlessly cruel to some.

I was given a photo of them all in a circle laughing as they did up the gowns on the big day and shared happiness was obvious. Three months later, Bride O died with all her family and her five bridesmaids present. They supported her to the end. I felt very privileged to have got to know them all, and to have shared the journey with them. There was courage and compassion and loyalty and so much love shared in this wedding. An example many could learn from.

Bride P was a local person known to me before she entered the shop. It was nice to hear she was marrying another local, whom I didn't know at the time. I did get to meet him one day when he dropped the bride outside the store. Bride O said he was a passionate fisherman and loved to go sailing with his Uncle on weekends. Laughing, she said that wouldn't happen after the wedding as she hated fishing and wouldn't be going boating with them. She didn't swim well and felt safer on shore. The wedding was to have a nautical theme which he was happy about. The bridesmaids were to be dressed in different shades of blue and green to reflect the ocean. Mum was to wear light yellow for the sun and had chosen the fabric and was getting it made specially. It sounded lovely as she described it. Bride P chose a gown of white chiffon with diagonal swathing on an extended diagonal bodice, with a soft full tulle skirt on the bottom which drifted into a small train at the back. She looked like a floating cloud as she walked.

Two weeks before the wedding day, the couple organized their separate wedding celebrations, The Groom had a few drinks with his best man and the groomsmen while having several games of snooker. He insisted on no mad Bucks party as he and his Uncle were heading out for a fishing trip in the Uncles new boat the following day. The Bride had an at-home hen party involving drinking and movies. Both were organized so there would not be any hungover members on the wedding day.

On the Sunday morning at 8.15 am Bride P received a call from the coastguard saying they had received a Mayday call from the Uncles boat. They hadn't been given coordinates as the call dropped out. They were organizing search and rescue by boat and air; in the known fishing spot the pair had used before. So began a three-day fruitless search for the missing pair. No sightings were made over hundreds of miles of ocean. Meantime the groom's mates felt they had to do something for their friend, so they hired a charter boat to search for themselves. One of the group remembered a recent conversation about a new fishing spot the Groom wanted to try some time, so acting on a hunch, they set out for the new spot location. THEY FOUND THE GROOM! Floating, delirious, very dehydrated, and very badly sunburnt, all alone.

The groom said later he had hung onto the Uncle for two days knowing he was dead, though fatigue had finally loosened his grip. It appeared that the boat had been broadsided by a rogue wave which had capsized it completely and very suddenly. Such grief for the Uncles family....... such relief for the families of the Bride and Groom.

The Groom was in the hospital for a week due to his state, but he insisted on being released for his wedding even though walking was painful due to his sunburnt condition. The wedding did go ahead and as I had been invited, I got to witness first-hand the joy on the Grooms face when he saw his bride coming to meet him. At the reception, I noticed the hugs and clustering of the groomsmen around their friend. I'm sure the Groom would not have been able to thank them enough for rescuing him. I hope the couple were able to live their lives with the courage and tenacity shown by the groom during his ordeal. If they have, I'm sure their marriage will have been wonderful.

CHAPTER SIX

Out of the Ordinary

Every day in a bridal shop is as unique as the people who walk through the front door. As consultants, we deal with all religions and their customs, with many diverse nationalities and languages, different requests and very often short time frames!

Bride Q entered my shop in bewilderment with her three granddaughters. They had just informed her that she was about to have her perfect wedding that day. I was informed that the Bride had been married 50 yrs. previously in a courthouse service. Her lovely granddaughters had decided to have a renewal of vows service on their anniversary and get grandmother dressed as a bride so she would have the full wedding experience.

In a whispered conversation they said their Grandfather was in the know, and he had spent three days writing up four pages to read to her about their love and marriage. They had got Grandmother to come to town by saying they were taking her out for a coffee. No wonder she had been bewildered when they entered my shop instead.

At the time we were dealing with two new customers in our dressing room who needed to come first as they had made appointments previously. However, the three young ones said it was urgent they get the gown sorted as the service was in *2 hours* and grandmother still had hair, makeup and nails to be done first.

Given the extremely short notice, we asked our current clients if we could share their time. We all thought it such a wonderful caring gesture by the young girls, and so all the people in the store joined in the fun of finding the perfect gown. It ended up being a cream crepe empire line gown with three-quarter sleeves which was accessorized with a little cream hat tilted on her head. The gown was a little long but with no time to alter the hem, Grandmother would have to wear shoes with a small heel. Bride Q still looked unsure, until she looked in the mirror and saw herself as a true bride! Her smile said it all and the hugs for the granddaughters showed her joy.

Some of us teared up with emotion, but we tried to be professional as we wished her well for her day,

Amazingly the whole visit only took an hour from when the clients entered and then left the store. We were all impressed with the granddaughter's treatment of their grandparents, and they were discussed and admired as we went back to helping our two booked-in brides. It was a really nice event to be part of, and I loved the photo of the couple that made it to my wall afterwards. I called that visit my One Hour Wedding.

Bride R came into the store three-quarters of an hour before closing on a Friday night. She said she wanted to buy a wedding gown that was soft and flowing and able to be packed up small! She explained that she and her partner had had a special Xmas holiday overseas for seven years, and she had hoped he would propose on every occasion. Tired of waiting, she had secretly organised a commitment ceremony to happen on the beach of the island location they were travelling to the following day!

The Groom would be informed of the ceremony at 10 am on their first morning there. Bride Q said it wouldn't of course be a real wedding, but it would still be a commitment by them, and a romantic memory. I agreed with her. We found her a simple straight-through chiffon gown that had a tiny train. In cream it featured a center gather right down the front that made the gown hug the body with soft swathing. As Bride R was a perfect size 12, she looked WOW with it on She said she would wear island fresh flowers in her hair on the day, The straps needed lifting and the hem needed shortening, so I said I could do the alterations overnight for her. She then asked if she could pick the gown up before the shop opened, as she had to catch a plane early. She also asked me to fold the gown as small as possible into a gift box and cover it with Xmas paper. That way it would look like a gift if her fiancé spotted it. I felt very disrespectful to the gown as I packed it tight into a box later that night.

Three weeks later Bride R rushed into the shop with the biggest smile and waved a very large engagement ring at me. Gleefully she told me her fiancé had officially proposed to her at midnight on the beach in front of their hotel under a full moon, and that he actually knelt to do it. Just hours before the commitment service was to happen. She said they were on cloud nine during that service on the day.

Now they were home she intended to have a proper full-on wedding, which would be legal and memorable also. She was going to have a different gown loaned by a friend, and she was so excited to be able to get married with family and friends present. I was excited for and with her. Secretly, though I never mentioned it, I was super happy that the proposal had pre-dated the first service. It would always prove to Bride R that he cared enough for her to want their marriage. Well, at least that's my perspective!

Bride S had definite ideas about her required wedding gown when she visited for the first time. She insisted it had to be *Red with a full train.* As this was a first-time wedding, I was intrigued about the colour choice. She explained they would be married overseas in winter, and she wanted a red gown to stand out against the snow she would be photographed in. The Groom was to wear black as were the bridesmaids. I could envision it as she spoke.

Bride S was in luck as I had two styles in store in red. One was a maroon red, the other fire engine red. Fire engine red won. The gown was an off-shoulder corset-boned top with a small decorative shoulder frill and a zipped back. The skirt was fully box pleated with a very long train. The edge of the train was also decorated with small frills. It looked amazing and the bride was happy to purchase it. I made a point of telling her that Indian brides wore red gowns as they believe it is lucky. She laughed on a subsequent visit as she told me that people were asking about the colour of her gown, and she was saying "It is red ". Nobody believed her until she turned up at the church on the wedding day.

The photos in the snow certainly were stunning, and Bride S looked lovely wearing a white short fur coat over her red gown. I'm sure the weather was cold enough to need it at the time. Their wedding photo stood out on the photo wall, and was studied by many that visited;

Bride T also ended up with a red wedding gown. She came in with her groom, who insisted he be allowed to view the choice of gowns available. He also stated he wanted to view the bride as she tried them on. Not the traditional bridal visit this time with bride, friends and family! Just the couple and no females present.

The groom expressed his opinion fully on gowns tried on, and commented that, as he was paying for the gown, he wanted a certain price point. The Bride said very little and didn't seem to be happy about her groom's comments. Eventually, the groom decided that they would purchase a strapless maroon-red gown, with a small skirt featuring pickups on it and without a train. He chose to buy the store sample and they then left the shop. I felt uneasy watching them leave as I wondered why the Bride would choose to marry such a dominating man.

A few months later Bride T entered the store carrying the wedding gown box and crying as she tried to explain why she was back. Her groom had decided to break the engagement off as he fancied someone else he said. He had informed Bride T she was to bring the gown back and get his money refunded. Bride T was distraught, so I took her out the back of the shop and made her a cup of tea. I listened as she confided in me how he had behaved towards her, and the word *bully* leapt into my mind.

When she had calmed down enough, I told her she had actually had a lucky escape. My opinion of him on his first visit had been that he was controlling and demanding. What she had just divulged had confirmed that opinion. I then went on to try to persuade her that her life would improve without him, and I assured her she was better off having discovered this about him before the wedding and not after,

Legally I didn't have to refund or take the gown back but for the Brides sake, I did. She was very grateful at the time for my understanding and help. I was grateful to see her escape an unhappy relationship and can only hope she chose more wisely in her future.

Bride U came into the shop with her two-year-old bonny baby boy on her hip and a very big smile. Her baby was so good-looking that he got more fuss initially from me than his mum. Bride U didn't mind, as she explained they had spent four years and 10,000 dollars on IVF to give birth to him. He was their miracle child, as she had been informed, she couldn't have children due to a medical condition. She hit the jackpot with the baby as he was such a happy child on all his visits to the store,

Bride U bought all the wedding attire through me, and I loved the visits with all her friends and family. About six months into the wedding schedule, she raced into the store one day to tell me she was pregnant again……. naturally. It was an unbelievable event no one ever thought would happen. Exciting as the news was, it caused a few problems in having to work out an estimated size she could expect to be with her pregnancy when the wedding rolled around. Then we had to work out if her chosen style of gown would be able to be adjusted to accommodate her baby bump. Then we would need drastic alterations at the latest possible moment before the wedding. Of course, it was sorted, and the wedding went on with the addition of a planned baby gender reveal, which showed they were having another boy. Nature continues to surprise us all.

Bride U possibly started a trend, as within a month of her new baby news, I had three successive current brides ring me with the news they were pregnant -all three in one week. No, they didn't know each other, hadn't attended any parties together or drunk the same water. It wasn't even Spring at the time.

Bride V was having a local wedding with a marriage celebrant from out of town, and the catering was being done in a local wedding venue. It was a wedding featuring 112 guests, who were also local. Preparations were all going well and as scheduled until the weather report showed a cyclone heading for the coast! It was hoped the cyclone would change course, as they often had in the past, so the wedding wasn't cancelled in the days before as expected, Torrential rain swept in and over the town two days before the wedding date and everyone watched and hoped the cyclone would change course.

Still, the wedding wasn't cancelled. Overnight before the wedding, the cyclone crossed land and massive destruction occurred. Trees were uprooted, roads flooded, some townships were cut off and total loss of power occurred in many areas. Streetlights weren't working, the rain was relentless with visibility limited on flooded roads and no street lighting to assist. The wedding went on as planned. The dance music was CDs played on battery-operated radios, as of course, the band hadn't turned up. Meantime the caterers had to hastily organize a barbeque wedding breakfast as power cuts were happening in the area. Due to that, the local venue had candles and torchlight only for the reception venue. Only about a quarter of the guests braved the elements to attend.

Most of the speeches were drowned out by the rain noise on the roof, and those people in attendance were obviously wishing to leave as soon as they decently could.

When the bride and groom were asked afterwards, by attendees, why they hadn't cancelled the wedding day the answer left them rather speechless. They were told the couple thought it would make their wedding different and more memorable. They would have a great story to tell people about their wedding day difference. Also, they wouldn't lose money due to the cancellation fees.

Ignorant of the forces of nature, they hadn't thought of injury, or even possible death for those that attended that day. I hope they gained more wisdom as their married life went on.

Brides W and X came into the store together to organize their wedding. They were in a long-term relationship, but the country we were in didn't allow Gay marriages. They had arranged a trip to Las Vegas and intended to be married by an Elvis impersonator in the little chapel on the strip. I was able to relate to their excitement as I had visited Las Vegas myself a decade before. It is truly a magical place to be. Of course, they would honeymoon there afterwards.

We had such a lot of laughs with both the girls as they had decided to purchase a gown each. We dressed them in side-by-side areas .and then pulled the curtain back for them to see each other and make comments. Such a lot of teasing occurred between them, which was lovely to see and hear. They were so happy together and it showed. When they collected their gowns some months later after the alterations were done, they promised to show us the photos of their wedding. We assured them with a smile that we would be studying their photos and not looking at Elvis.

True to their word, a couple of months later the girls came into the store with their wedding album. We were between appointments, so we had an hour to chat and check out the photos. Ironically our country had passed a law allowing same sex marriages to be legally recognized just one week before. When I asked if they wished they could have been married at home with friends and family, the answer was a quick NO! Las Vegas was their dream wedding- though they had thrown a massive party on their return for those who weren't there on the actual day. Of course, Elvis's music was played that night as well.

Bride Y was a woman of very slim build, tall, with an olive complexion and shoulder length naturally dark hair. She was very very attractive, and though not young, I couldn't have guessed her age correctly. She said she was looking to try on a particular style and showed me the photo of it. I didn't have the gown in store, but said I was happy to show her two gowns that would let her get an idea if the style was right for her. They were of course too big as she was a tiny size 4 but I juggled them to fit. We were both happy that the style would suit and, fortunately, I purchased off that particular supplier. She ordered her gown through me that day and booked her bridesmaids in for their gown selection appointment.

I learned that she had been with her fiancé for many years, they had five children together, they had invested in rental properties successfully and had just done a world cruise! The only experience left was to get married so hence her shopping. I was incredulous at the five children admission, given her lovely figure and good looks. She really didn't look old enough to me.

Over time she spared no expense with purchases for the wedding and was so pleasant to deal with throughout all visits, I was amazed at the high heel Jimmy Choo shoes she purchased for the day, as they were completely covered in Swarovski crystals and the sparkle when she moved was amazing. The cost for them? Over 6000 dollars. The final splash out for the wedding was that they had rented a CASTLE in Germany and would have the wedding service and reception there. A true fairytale wedding, which went without a hitch on the day

I was sent a usb stick containing a video covering the whole day immediately after the wedding. It was fantastic to view. Then Bride Y came into the store with a special wall photo for me. While thanking me for providing a wonderful wedding experience, she told me something else. Her first wedding experience was to enter a very high-end bridal store in the city with her photo to ask for assistance.

The owner looked her over and apparently told her, rather rudely, that she was wasting her time as they wouldn't have anything to fit her! As she wasn't offered any assistance, she left the store immediately. I thought of the price she had paid to me for the Haute Couture wedding gown and fancy accessories, and for the bridesmaids as well. Also, the special cuff links for the groomsmen and Groom, and Mums outfit and special jewelry. The total cost ran into thousands, and my store was the beneficiary. One high end sale was completely missed in the city. A true-life Pretty Women moment!

TIMES ARE A CHANGING.
A NEW LEARNING EXPERIENCE

Three decades have seen such an accelerated amount of change in everyone's lives. So too has the Bridal industry been changed. From the moral codes of expected virginal brides, we now have long-term unmarried couples who have lived together for years and who have children to include in the ceremony. We have a recognized Rainbow community and now Transgender people. Mixed-race marriages are normal now, whereas once they were taboo. Multi-cultural communities have also introduced their wedding customs to others. Priests will now also hold wedding services, with papal approval of course, outside of the catholic church's traditional services.

Wedding vows are written nowadays by the bride and groom themselves, and ceremonies are held in strange places and often in themed costumes. We have commitment ceremonies as well, instead of legal marriages. We also occasionally have vow renewal services which have been sometimes followed by a family christening immediately afterwards. We have same-sex couples using surrogacy to become parents. There has been an astonishing amount of change.

I believe there has also been, in this process, more acceptance, tolerance, understanding, and love. May this continue always.

Thank you, Dear reader, for travelling this far with me. I hope you enjoyed the read. Till we meet again, peace and blessings to you all, as you have now reached *the end.*